The Umbrella Theory

"Every relationship has its place
Under your umbrella,
Beside it,
Or outside it.
Wisdom is knowing the difference"

Published By Umbrella Press
Green Cove Springs, FL
ISBN: 979-8-9955389-1-2
Printed in the United States of America

A Reflection on Family,
Responsibility, and Boundaries

Jamie Garrison

Most families are not missing love.
They are missing umbrellas.

An umbrella defines responsibility.

It protects what belongs beneath it. ☂

When rain falls on a family, it rarely falls evenly.
Sometimes the storm is loud.
Money problems.
Sickness.
Uncertainty about the future.

Sometimes the storm is quiet.
Misunderstandings.
Unspoken expectations.
Advice that was meant kindly but felt like pressure.

Differences in belief.
Differences in faith.
Differences in how children should be raised.

Families rarely break because they lack love.

More often, they break because responsibility becomes unclear.

Lines blur.
Roles shift.
Boundaries fade.

And slowly, without anyone intending it, the rain begins to reach places it was never meant to reach.

Many families struggle with a simple question.
Who is responsible for what?

Parents guiding adult children.
Adult children seeking permission.
Grandparents stepping into roles that belong to parents.

Everyone caring.
Everyone trying to help.
And yet, somehow, everyone stepping on each other.

Again, the problem is not love.
The problem is confusion.
Confusion about responsibility.
Confusion about boundaries.

And when that confusion grows, families begin to feel the rain. ☂

Without boundaries, relationships begin to tangle.

The rain reaches places it was never meant to reach.

Advice becomes interference.
Concern becomes control.

Good intentions begin to feel like pressure.

And pressure, even when it comes from love, can damage what it was meant to protect.

Healthy families understand something simple.

When the rain begins to fall,
they know where the umbrellas belong.

Each generation must eventually raise its own umbrella.

And each umbrella must be respected. ☂

When a man and woman marry, something important happens.

A new umbrella rises.

Under that umbrella lives their marriage.
Their decisions.
Their struggles.
Their victories.
Their way of building a home together.

This space belongs to them.
No parent stands there.
No friend directs it.
No outside voice controls it.

It is theirs to hold, and theirs to protect. ☂

Parents may still love them.
Friends may still support them.
Family may still offer advice.
But no one stands beneath that umbrella unless invited.

The umbrella protects the marriage.

Even from the people who raised them.
Because when two people marry, they do not simply join families.

They begin their own.

And that new family must learn to stand beneath its own umbrella. ☂

Before that moment, parents carry the umbrella.
For years they hold it high.

Beneath it, children grow learning what life is.

Parents' guide them.

Correct them.
Protect them.

They shape the direction of the home.

They teach what is right.
They teach what is wrong.

They show what responsibility looks like.

That umbrella belongs to them.

And the responsibility for what grows beneath it is theirs. ☂

No one else decides how those children are raised.

Not neighbors.
Not friends.
Not even grandparents.

The parents hold the umbrella.

The children grow beneath it.

The lessons are taught there.
The values are formed there.

Every strong family begins this way. ☂

Parenting is not only about protection.

It is about preparation.

The goal is not to keep children under the umbrella forever.

The goal is to prepare them to raise their own.

To stand in the rain.
To carry responsibility.

To hold an umbrella of their own. ☂

Children notice more than parents realize.

They see how parents speak to one another.
They see how disagreements are handled.

They see how forgiveness works.

They see whether respect is real or only spoken.
They see whether love is patient.
They see whether responsibility is carried.

These quite moments teach more than words.

And one day those lessons become the umbrella they hold for their own family. ☂

And eventually that day comes.

Children grow up.
They become adults.

They build relationships of their own.
They make decisions for themselves.

And one day, they marry.

And when they do, something important happens.

At that moment, a new umbrella rises.

The child who once stood beneath protection now carry its responsibility.

Their marriage becomes their space.
Their decisions become their own.

Their struggles become theirs to face together.
Their victories become theirs to celebrate together.

This is where independence begins.

This is where a new family learns to stand beneath its own umbrella. ☂

Parents often struggle with this moment.

Not because they wish harm.
Not because they lack love.
But because letting go is losing influence.

It can feel like stepping into a storm.

Yet healthy families understand something important.

Letting a child raise their own umbrella is not losing them.

It is allowing them to grow.

It is allowing them to become responsible for their own shelter. ☂

The relationship between parent and adult child does not disappear.

It changes shape.

Authority gives way to respect.
Direction gives way to support.
Control gives way to trust.

A new umbrella rises.

And healthy families grow stronger when parents and children recognize that shift. ☂

Faith and the Umbrella

Faith often lives close to the heart of a family.

It shapes how parents pray.
How children learn about God.
How a home speaks about right and wrong.

For many parents, faith becomes one of the deepest gifts they pass down. ☂

While children grow beneath the family umbrella, parents teach what they believe.

They take their children to church.
They share their understanding of God.
They model what faith looks like in daily life.

These lessons become part of the foundation
children will carry beneath their own umbrella one day. ☂

But when children grow up
and raise umbrellas of their own,
something important changes.

Their faith journey becomes their faith journey.

They may attend the same church.
They may choose another.
They may practice differently than they were raised.

That decision now belongs under their umbrella. ☂

Parents may still share their beliefs.
They may still pray for their children.
They may still speak about their faith.

But faith cannot be forced across umbrellas.

It must be chosen beneath one's own. ☂

Respecting another umbrella
means allowing space for that choice.

Judgment closes doors.
Pressure creates distance.

But respect leaves room
for relationships to remain strong.

Even when paths look different. ☂

Conflict Between Umbrellas

Sometimes umbrellas collide.

Parents overstep into a marriage.
Adult children reject the guidance
of those that raised them.
Grandparents attempt to direct homes that are no longer theirs.

These moments create tension.

Not because love has disappeared.
But because umbrellas have been crossed. ☂

Healthy families learn to step back when this happens.

They remember where their umbrella belongs.

They return to their responsibility.

And they respect the space
that belongs to others.

When Someone Refuses the Umbrella

Not every relationship follows the ideal path.

Sometimes someone steps away.
Sometimes someone refuses connection.
Sometimes distance grows between umbrellas.

These moments are painful.

But they are part of the storms
many family faces. ☂

You cannot force someone
to stand beneath your umbrella.

You cannot control
every relationship.

But you can remain faithful
to the responsibility that is yours.

Protect what is under your care.

Maintain the relationships you can.

Leave space for reconciliation
if the storm passes. ☂

The truth is simple.

A person cannot control the weather of life.
Storms arrive without warning.

But each person can decide
what stands beneath their umbrella.

Their marriage.
Their children.
Their commitments.
Their character. ☂

Strong families are not built
by everyone controlling one another.

They are built when each person understands
where their umbrella belongs.

And stands there faithfully.

Even when the rain begins to fall. ☂

Every family carries an umbrella.

Some hold it well.
Some are still learning.
Some are rebuilding.

If this idea has touched your life—
if it has challenged you, or changed how
you see your family—

The idea continues through
the stories of families.

I would like to hear your story. ☂

mystory@theumbrellatheory.org

Not all books are meant to be kept.
Some are meant to be read, read again, and then passed on.

If the ideas in this book speak to you, adopt its philosophy. Then share the value of what you've learned with someone else.

Umbrellas grow stronger when they cover more people.

THEORY

www.ingramcontent.com/pod-product-compliance
Lightning Source LLC
LaVergne TN
LVHW090541110826
845146LV00003B/1213

* 9 7 9 8 9 9 5 5 3 8 9 1 2 *